"Dogs are the leaders of the planet. If you see two life forms, one of them's making a poop, the other one's carrying it for him, who would you assume is in charge?"

— Jerry Seinfeld

A is for Armadillo

Armadillo means "little armored **one**."
If you smell their poop, your nose won't have **fun**!

B is for Beaver

Beavers are rodents; they eat trees and **bark**.
They stay up at night and poop in the **dark**!

C is for Cat

A cat poops more than thirty pounds a **year**.
That's so much poo-poo coming from its **rear**!

D is for Dog

Some dogs poop outside and some on a **pad**,
yet all dogs have poop that smells very **bad**!

E is for Elephant

Elephants use their trunks to take **showers**;
they shower after making poo **towers**!

F is for Fly

Flies potty almost every time they **land**.
Watch out when you have ice cream in your **hand**!

G is for Green Humphead Parrot Fish

Green Humphead Parrot Fish poo sand, it's **true**.
They make beautiful beaches just for **you**!

H is for Hippo

Hippos use their tails to make poop **scatter**,
it's like a fan that makes poo-poo **splatter**!

I is for Ibex

An ibex is a wild mountain **goat**,
dropping poop in places high and **remote**.

J is for Jerboa

Jerboas are rodents that hop and **skip**.
They poop so fast it's over in a **zip**!

K is for Komodo Dragon

Komodo Dragons' poop smells so so **bad**,
just one whiff will make your nose so so **mad**!

L is for Llama

The best smelling poop comes from a **llama**,
it does its business without much **drama**.

M is for Mandrill

Mandrills' bright red butts just can't be **beaten**;
when they poop, you'll wonder what they've **eaten**!

N is for Narwhal

Narwhals like to travel in great big **groups**;
the bigger the groups, the bigger the **poops**!

O is for Owl

Owls poop butt nuggets and also **vomit**.
Waste ejects out of them like a **comet**.

P is for Penguin

Adélie penguins poo at a fast **pace**,
so much pink poop it can be seen from **space**!

Q is for Quoll

Quolls poop more when they want to find a **date**,
they use the terrible smell as love **bait**!

R is for Rabbit

Rabbits sometimes eat their own bottom **waste**,
it gives good gut flora and a bad **taste**!

S is for Sloth

Sloths always look like they're wearing big **smiles**.
They poop just once a week, making big **piles**!

T is for Turkey Vulture

Turkey Vultures poop themselves when they're **warm**,
cooling their legs with a smelly poo **storm**.

U is for Unicorn

Unicorn poop is magical, you **know**!
It goes through the clouds and turns into **snow**!

V is for Vampire Bat

Vampire bats get their food with a quick **bite**,
they lap blood up and poop it out at **night**.

W is for Wombat

Wombats have butt bones that make their scat **square**.
They poop through the night, stinking up the **air!**

X is for X-Ray Tetra

X-ray tetras are fish you can see **through**.
Look close enough, and you can see their **poo**!

Y is for Yellowjacket

Yellowjackets eat bugs and aphid **poop**.
These yellow wasps turn it into white **goop**.

Z is for Zorilla

Zorillas use poop and their anal **glands**
to keep others away and mark their **lands**.

ALSO AVAILABLE

F IS FOR FART (PICTURE BOOK)

F IS FOR FART (HANDWRITING ACTIVITY BOOK)

F IS FOR FART (COLORING BOOK)

A IS FOR AVIATION (PICTURE BOOK)

A IS FOR AVIATION (HANDWRITING ACTIVITY BOOK)